Easter: The Everlasting Story

The illustrations in this book were selected from
The Lion Bible: Everlasting Stories, published by
Lion Hudson in 2001

Text by Lois Rock
Illustrations copyright © 2001 Christina Balit
This edition copyright © 2004 Lion Hudson

A Lion Children's Book
an imprint of
Lion Hudson plc
Mayfield House, 256 Banbury Road,
Oxford OX2 7DH, England
www.lionhudson.com
ISBN 0 7459 4744 1

First edition 2004
3 5 7 9 10 8 6 4 2

A catalogue record for this book is available
from the British Library

Typeset in 16/22 Lapidary 333 BT
Printed and bound in Singapore

EASTER
The Everlasting Story

Retold by Lois Rock
Illustrated by Christina Balit

LION
Children's Books

One springtime, long ago, everyone was talking about Jesus of Nazareth.

'He is a wonderful storyteller,' said the children.

'He welcomes everybody,' said the outcasts.

'We believe he can work miracles,' added those who were sick.

'But how can the son of a carpenter be a teacher?' asked the religious leaders. 'Who is this Jesus? Who can he be?'

'Someone who has changed our world,' said Jesus' followers.
'He speaks of God's love for us all, and God's forgiveness.'

Among those whose lives had been most changed were Jesus'
twelve disciples – Jesus' special friends, who were helping to build
God's kingdom on earth. Closest to Jesus were the fishermen
Peter and John, who had left everything they knew to follow him.

It was the time of the great Jewish festival of Passover. People were travelling from all over the world to Jerusalem and the Temple there.

'And so must we,' said Jesus to his disciples. He asked two of them to go and fetch a donkey and her colt for him to ride the last part of the journey.

As Jesus rode along the road that leads down the Mount of Olives to Jerusalem, other travellers began to notice.

'It's Jesus,' they said to one another. 'He's riding to the city that great King David of old made his own. Riding, not walking. Perhaps that's a sign Jesus is God's new king...'

Some took their cloaks off and threw them on the ground for the donkey to walk on. Others cut palm branches and waved them in the air like banners.

People began shouting:

'Praise to the son of our great King David!'

'God bless the king who comes in the name of the Lord!'

Among the crowd were some religious leaders. They did not like what they were hearing. As Jesus passed by, they gathered to whisper and to plan.

In the Temple courtyard, everyone was busy with preparations for the Passover festival. Pilgrims were buying the special coins for making their offerings. There were animals for people to buy as sacrifices: lambs and calves and pigeons. The air was filled with shouting and arguing.

Jesus watched, and suddenly he grew angry. He grabbed some cord and knotted it into a whip.

'Get out!' he ordered a stallholder, flicking the whip.

The stallholder fell back in surprise.

Jesus walked to another stall piled high with coins and tipped it over. Coins jingled to the ground and rolled in circles.

'Get out!' shouted Jesus. 'Buying and selling and cheating has nothing to do with the worship of God. The Temple is meant to be a house of prayer. You are making it a den of thieves.'

He sent another stall crashing and then another. In the hubbub, children ran, pigeons flew about in a panic and animals stampeded. The Temple officials came running.

'How dare you do this,' said one to Jesus.

'The man's mad,' said another official. 'We'll have to do something to get rid of him.'

After that, and for several days, Jesus continued to teach the crowds. He told them of the right way to live as true friends of God.

Meanwhile, his enemies were putting their plans together. They were delighted when one of Jesus' disciples, Judas Iscariot, came to visit them. 'We will pay you thirty pieces of silver if you help us find Jesus when the crowds who love him aren't with him,' they said, and the secret deal was done.

Soon the other disciples were busy with Passover celebrations. When all was ready, they gathered around a table in an upstairs room for a special meal.

At the table, Jesus took a piece of bread, gave thanks to God, broke it, and gave it to his disciples. He said, 'This is my body, which is given for you. Do this in memory of me.'

After supper, he gave them a cup of wine. He said, 'This cup is God's new covenant, an agreement sealed with my blood, which is poured out for you.'

There was a pause. In the silence, Jesus said, 'Look! The person who is going to betray me is here at the table with me.'

'What does he mean?' Peter whispered to John.

'Who does he mean?' murmured John. Then all the disciples began to talk and to argue.

'And you, Peter,' said Jesus, 'you need to know that testing times are ahead. I have prayed that your faith will not fail. When you turn back to me, you must help the others.'

'I'll never turn away from you,' Peter protested.

Jesus sighed. 'Before the cock crows at the end of this night, you will have said three times that you do not know me.'

In the dark of the night, Jesus and his disciples went to a shady grove on the Mount of Olives. The disciples fell asleep, but Jesus spent the long hours praying to God.

'Father,' he said, 'take this cup of suffering away from me. Yet it is not what I want that must be done, but what you want.'

Then he went back to the sleeping disciples. 'Get up now,' he urged, 'and pray for strength.'

As he spoke, Judas appeared in the shadows. Behind him came a band of soldiers. Judas greeted Jesus with a kiss... but it was really a sign to the soldiers. They arrested him and marched him to the house of the high priest.

The other disciples ran away, but Peter followed at a distance. As the door slammed on Jesus, Peter sat outside in the courtyard. A servant girl came past.

'I know that man,' she said, peering at Peter's face. 'He's one of Jesus' followers.'

'I don't even know him!' retorted Peter.

A little while later, a man came by. 'You're one of Jesus' followers, aren't you?' he said.

'No, I am not!' Peter insisted.

An hour went by. The sky paled as dawn approached. Peter found himself drawn into talking with the servants.

'I can tell by your accent that you're from Galilee,' said one. 'You're one of Jesus' disciples.'

'I don't know what you're talking about,' cursed Peter.

It was then that Jesus was hustled out. Peter stood up. A cock crowed. Jesus turned and looked straight at Peter.

And Peter wept.

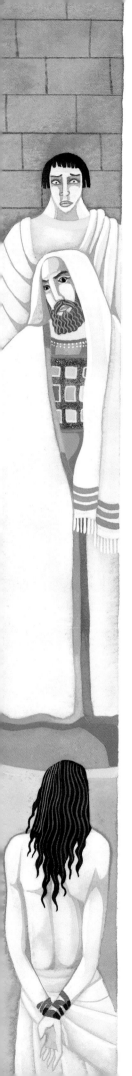

When day came, the religious leaders and the chief priests met to question Jesus.

'Are you God's chosen king,' they asked, 'the Messiah of whom the prophets spoke?'

Jesus would not give a clear yes or a clear no. 'We can make our own judgment on this,' they said, and they took Jesus to stand trial before the Roman governor, Pontius Pilate.

'This man has been misleading our people,' they told him. 'He has been telling them not to pay taxes to the Roman emperor. He claims that he is our people's Messiah, which means king.'

Pilate tried to make sense of the accusations. Then he called everyone together. 'I do not see that there is any serious charge against Jesus,' he said. 'I shall have him whipped and then I shall let him go.'

'Be careful,' warned Jesus' accusers. 'The crowd will not like that.'

The crowd was part of their plan. When Pilate asked if he should release Jesus as a favour at the festival, they asked for a criminal instead. 'And what of Jesus?' asked Pilate.

'Crucify him! Crucify him!' chanted the mob. The mood was angry, and Pilate began to fear a riot.

'Very well then,' he said. He took some water and washed his hands in front of them. 'I am not responsible for the death of this man,' he announced. 'It is your doing.'

Soldiers led Jesus away, along with two criminals who had also been condemned to death. On a hillside just outside the city, they nailed each of them to a cross of wood. Above Jesus was a sign: 'This is the king of the Jews.'

Jesus did not curse or struggle. He said a prayer: 'Forgive them, Father! They don't know what they are doing.'

As Jesus hung on the cross, he saw his mother, tears of grief streaming down her face. John stood next to her, his face creased with misery.

'There is your son now,' Jesus said to Mary. To his friend he said, 'There is your mother.'

Jesus suffered for three long, dark hours. Then, with a cry, he died.

One of the religious leaders named Joseph had not wanted Jesus put to death.

But all Joseph could do now was offer a decent burial. He owned a tomb cut out of solid rock, and went to Pilate to ask if he could take Jesus' body.

Some of the women who had been followers of Jesus stood by as the body of Jesus was wrapped in linen and laid on a ledge in the tomb. They watched as the stone door was rolled in place. But the sun was setting and the weekly day of rest was beginning. As they hurried away, they agreed to return another day to wrap the body properly with spices and perfumes.

Very early on the day after the sabbath, they came back.

'Who will roll back the stone for us?' they asked as they walked along. 'It is very heavy.'

To their amazement, the door was already open. They walked in, then gasped in sudden fear: sitting on the ledge was a young man dressed in white.

'Don't be alarmed,' he said. ' I know you are looking for Jesus of Nazareth, who was crucified. He is not here – he is risen from the dead. Now go and tell his disciples that he going to Galilee and will meet them there.'

The women ran away, terrified.

When Peter and John heard their news, they went running to see. Peter rushed straight in, and John followed.

The first rays of sunlight shone into the cave. On the ledge were the linen wrappings, but no sign of Jesus. Puzzled and unhappy, they went away.

Mary Magdalene stayed by the tomb, crying. She bent down to look into the tomb one more time. Two angels dressed in white were sitting in the very place where the body should have been.

'Why are you crying?' they asked.

'They have taken the body of my Lord, and I do not know where they have put him.'

Something made her turn round. A man was standing among the olive trees. She thought he must be the gardener.

'Sir, if you are the one who took him away, please tell me where you put him, so I can go and get him,' she pleaded.

The man bent closer towards her. 'Mary!' he said.

'Teacher!' she whispered, and reached out her hands.

'Do not hold on to me,' Jesus said, 'because I have not yet gone back up to the Father. But go to my brothers and tell them that I am returning to him who is my Father and their Father, who is my God and their God.'

So Mary went and told the disciples that she had seen Jesus.

The disciples were puzzled by Mary's news. They could only sit and wonder about what was happening. No one dared go around asking questions – they were all afraid that the authorities would be searching for them. Only Thomas had even dared step out of the place where they were now hiding.

Then Jesus came and stood among them. 'Peace be with you,' he said. He went on to explain that it was now their job to continue the work that he had begun.

Suddenly, mysteriously, he was gone. Thomas returned to find his friends in an exuberant mood. 'We have seen the Lord!' they said. 'Jesus was here in this room.'

'You must be imagining it,' Thomas replied scornfully. 'Jesus was dead. I won't believe that you saw him unless I see him. I want to see the nail marks in his hands and the wound where the soldiers put a spear in his side.'

A week later, when everyone was together in the room with the doors locked, Jesus came again.

He spoke to Thomas. 'Here are my hands,' he said. 'See the marks. Touch my side. Stop your doubting, and believe!'

Thomas replied, 'My Lord and my God!'

In the days that followed, some of Jesus' disciples made their way back home to Galilee.

'I'm going fishing,' said Peter.

The others went with him. All night long they trawled their nets through the dark water, but they did not catch anything. As dawn came, they headed back to shore.

A man waved to them from the beach. 'Have you caught anything?'

'No! A wasted night!' they replied.

The man called again. 'Throw the net out to the right of the boat.'

They did so. At once, the net was full of fish. 'We can't get all these on board,' they gasped as they tugged on the ropes.

John was looking at the man on the shore. 'It's Jesus,' he whispered to Peter.

At that, Peter jumped into the water and swam to shore, leaving the others to haul the boat in, the heavy net trailing behind.

Jesus had a charcoal fire burning and some fresh bread.

'Bring some of your fish here,' he said, and he prepared a meal for them all.

Afterwards, Jesus spoke to Peter alone. 'Do you love me more than these others do?'

'Yes, Lord,' he answered, 'you know that I love you.'

Jesus asked the question a second time, and a third. 'Lord, you know everything, you know that I love you,' the disciple replied.

'Take good care of my sheep,' said Jesus; and he asked Peter to be loyal once again and to take care of his followers, whatever the cost.

Jesus appeared to his disciples for forty days. He reminded them of everything that he had taught them about God's kingdom, which exists wherever people live as God's friends. He told them to spread the message of the kingdom to the entire world.

'But wait for a little while,' he said, 'for God will give you the Holy Spirit to help you.'

As he was speaking, Jesus was taken up into heaven, and a cloud hid him from their sight.

They were still looking at the sky when two men dressed in
white appeared.

'Why are you standing there looking up at the sky?' they asked.
'This Jesus, who was taken from you into heaven, will come back
in the same way that you saw him go.'

Ten days later came the festival called Pentecost. All the people who believed in Jesus were together in Jerusalem, still hiding, still fearful.

Suddenly, there was a noise from the sky – like the sound of a rushing wind. They looked around and saw what looked like flames dancing out to touch each person there, filling them with joy and laughter. Words bubbled up inside them – words of praise to God, but in different languages they had never learned.

They rushed out into the street, talking to pilgrims from all over the world in the different languages God had enabled them to speak.

'What's going on?' people asked one another. 'Are these people drunk?'

Peter stood up, as bold and fearless as he had ever been. 'These people are not drunk,' he said, 'it's far too early in the morning for that. No – what you see are people filled with God's Holy Spirit. We are followers of Jesus – the one who was crucified and whom I declare has been raised from the dead. He is the Messiah, the one sent by God to save us.

'So turn away from all your wrongdoing and make a new start: be baptized in the name of Jesus. God will welcome you and forgive you. You will be God's friends, God's own children.'

In this way, Peter began the work of spreading the message of Jesus: the message to bring people into God's everlasting kingdom.

More Easter books from
Lion Children's Books

The Lion Bible: Everlasting Stories   *Lois Rock and Christina Balit*

The Easter Angels   *Bob Hartman and Tim Jonke*

The Story of the Cross   *Mary Joslin and Gail Newey*

The Tale of Three Trees   *Angela Elwell Hunt and Tim Jonke*